THE BUMPER BOOK OF
CARTOONS

THE BUMPER BOOK OF
CARTOONS

Arthur Barker Limited   London
A subsidiary of Weidenfeld (Publishers) Limited

ISBN 0 213 16884 7

Filmset by Deltatype, Ellesmere Port
Printed in Great Britain by
Butler & Tanner Ltd., Frome and London

For Victoria and Emma

CITROËN 2CV

Elle driver

Not all 2CV's are driven by vegetarian potters called Harriet, but research shows that 82% are. Harriet lives in West Hampstead, goes to picture-framing classes, smokes Disque Bleu, and has a *live-in lover* called Sean, who can't drive, but can play the guitar.

So popular have the NUCLEAR POWER – NO THANKS stickers become on 2CV's, that they are now being applied at the factory, in a choice of four European languages. They are sometimes supplemented with a CRUISE OUT, or STOP THE BLOODY WHALING, but the latter tends to be found more often on the Renault 4.

On long journeys, particularly on the M4 on their way to stay with some self-sufficient fellow-ecologists in South Wales, overtaking manoeuvres have to be worked out, sometimes miles ahead. This is second nature to the experienced *Deuche* driver, and Harriet would have no other; TWO HORSE-POWER – YES PLEASE. To the uninitiated, the sight of a 2CV cornering can be somewhat alarming, but they very rarely fall over. When one does, it becomes à Citroën pressée.

RENAULT 5

Le Car

In honour of the number of Carolines who drive these trendy little runabouts, Renault named this model after her and called it **Le Car.** Every weekday **Le Car** drops off **les children** at **le play-school** and heads **straight** for Sloane Square; there it is double-parked behind Peter Jones while Caroline **nips in** to quickly look at materials for the spare bedroom. After an hour or so of this, she drives up Sloane Street, stopping fleetingly at General Trading, and heads for Harrods. She buys dinner for eight that evening on her account, ('Roger's boss, **frightful** wife, but thank **God** Buffy and Charles are coming.')

Having loaded up, she whizzes round the corner to Beauchamp Place, where she skilfully squeezes into a space two inches shorter than **Le Car,** outside the restaurant where she is meeting two other Carolines for a **quick bite.** At half past three she exclaims, 'My goodness, is that the time. I simply **must** dash.' After popping into Caroline Charles to buy a blouse ('But **Darling,** I had absolutely **nothing** to wear.'), she speeds her way homewards, the long way, via Osborne and Little, Paperchase, and Walton Street, with one last **little peek** into Peter Jones before picking up the children. By the time Caroline actually reaches home, **Le Car** has attracted so many parking tickets, the windscreen looks like a school notice-board.

BMW 323i

Danny is a hyperactive account executive in his early thirties but with the worldly-wise demeanour, and blood pressure, of a fifty-year-old. He dresses as though he stepped straight from Cecil Gee's window display, and his hair-style suggests a photograph in an East End barber's shop. He is a constant blur of finger-clicking, gold jewellery and cuff-shooting.

He burns up a lot of his boundless energy by darting in and out of traffic, taking great pains and risks to be in the fastest-moving lane at all times. In Germany this is called 'winning Hans down'. Unfortunately, what seems a dead cert often turns out to be an also-ran. As with the Post Office queue the shortest is not necessarily the quickest; in the same way as the little old lady next in line decides to cash in her Granny Bonds, her Premium Bonds, her National Savings, send a bulky parcel to Sierra Leone, pick up her pension *and* pay for her television licence in five-pence pieces – so the little yellow Mini in the inside lane, signalling left, decides impulsively to turn right instead, and then stalls, leaving Danny, by now apoplectic, snookered behind the yellow. Just as Danny sees an opening, the lights change to red and the Mini decides to go straight on after all, and caterpaults forward, leaving him fuming on the grid. All this makes him very cross. One of his greatest frustrations is expending 300 joules (1 joule is equivalent to moving 1 Bmw through 1 metre of heavy traffic at sea-level) to be first on to the motorway, only to find that the little yellow Mini is once again alongside him.

Der Car

MORRIS 1000 TRAVELLER

Half-timbered Tudor

Janie is a fairly typical lesbian Buddhist one-parent Marxist separatist who teaches weaving and patchwork quilting at the Adult Institute. She is organizing a claimants-union-against-the-bomb summer camp for like-thinking soul-mates and has protested about most things since she was pushed in a pram by her father all the way from Aldermaston to London in the early fifties: cruise, Miss World, police brutality, South African oranges, Mexican grapes, seals, whales, Free Wales, dolphins and seat-belts. She is an occasional producer of one-act plays for the Gay Rastafarian Sweatshop and has written the odd gem about sapphic love on the dole in Belfast.

She regards the upsurge of interest in the Woody with some derision. 'Why don't those bloody middle-class trendies stick to their flashy little French cars.' Her Mother Courage outfit either came off the loom at the Institute or from jumble sales.

As Janie is something of a mechanical fundamentalist, the Morris's instrumentation (a cross between frugality and functionalism), suits her admirably. 'All you need to know, after all, is how fast you are going, how far you have gone, how much petrol you have left, and the name of the manufacturer.'

VOLVO ESTATE

Yes, I KNOW my lights are on

Manual or Dogmatic

Although Henry finds all those flashing warning lights a little irritating, he knows they do make sense. He chose a Volvo because it is the quintessential all-round safety-fast, school-running, point-to-pointing, two-labrador estate. He could, of course, have had a Fjord Granada Estate for the same sort of money, but most people still regard the Volvo as a more expensive car.

Once he has put the two children, Bartholomew and Cassandra, in the back and the matching dogs behind the wire grill, or occasionally vice versa, and has been told to fasten his, and his wife Annabel's seat-belts, make doubly sure all the doors are closed firmly, extinguish his cigarette, put in the choke and release the hand-brake, he sets off, safe in the knowledge that the only harm they could come to would be through an act of God, or by running head-on into another Volvo.

A lot of Henry's antique-dealer friends now have Volvos (although there was a time when they thought that it was part of the female genitalia). The safety-crazed Swedes are bringing out a device to be standard equipment on all their cars: if a sensor in the car detects more than 30mg of alcohol on the driver's breath, all the doors automatically lock, the car is rendered immobile with the driver trapped inside, and, through a loudspeaker system, calls the police in an hysterical voice. Henry may well choose another marque for his next car.

FORD CORTINA

The Cortina driver can easily be recognized by four main points; • he is driving three feet from your rear bumper; • he is flashing his lights; • his Harry Fenton polyester/cotton mix light grey jacket is hanging on hook behind him; • he is picking his nose. His name is Tel and he is late for a marketing meeting in Swindon.

He normally drives with one hand anyway, and in traffic jams, when not drumming his fingers on the roof, he is hammering out Diana Ross Chartbusters on the steering wheel. 'In Car Sounds' are more important to him than what's under the bonnet; he has a quartz-synthesized phase-lock looped stereo tuner with two door-mounted cross-axial speakers and a pair of 60-watt rear-shelf-located low-distortion two-way woofers, which he takes with him when he is given a newer model. Like the size of a civil servant's desk, Tel's success can be gauged by the size of his engine, and the number of letters after 'Cortina'. He now stands at 2.0GL and he is dreading being given a Sierra. 'Leave it aht, John, that's not a proper mower. What's wrong with the old Cortina?

Tel has a pair of miniature football boots dangling from the rear-view mirror, and he plays with the lads every Sunday morning. Saturdays he usually goes to watch West Ham get beaten at home.

Wholly Representative

MGBGT

NQOCD

It's not only air-hostesses who drive MGs. Most evenings Hooray Henry and his old school chum, Cheers Charlie, meet at the Admiral Cod for a drink. They both drive MGBs. Charlie sails on the Hamble at weekends, which explains the blue Guernsey over the striped shirt he wore to the auction house, where he works, but not necessarily the cheesecutter cap. Henry, on the other hand, plays rugger for the Old Boys, and although he owns a blue Guernsey, he prefers to wear a sports jacket, striped shirt and thick woolly tie in the evenings. Each Saturday his fiancée, Lucinda, loyally supports him by standing on the touchline wearing his Barbour and old school scarf. His car was a twenty-first birthday present from his parents. Charlie had to buy his from his earnings (with a little help from his Dad).

'Good drop of bitter, this. Mind you, had some Wadsworth 6X at the weekend. That takes some beating. Come on, sup up. We'll go round to Ginny's and pick Lucy up on the way.' At the Surprise, Charlie and Henry soon have the girls in stitches with their word-for-word re-enactments of Monty Python sketches. 'I know, let's have a quickie back at the Cod and then get some scoff. Yaah!'

Later, in the Bistro Vino, over a steak au poivre and bottle of undrinkable Armenian red, the boys' talk turns to cars, (Porsche versus Ferrari) and the girls name-drop-swap about skiing (Verbier versus Val d'Isère). After a repeat, by popular request, of the 'Parrot' sketch, they trundle off to their respective girl-friend's flats for a spot of car-door slamming and heavy petting.

BMW 635CSi

Ottomobile

Michael suffers from an acute superiority complex. He drives with an air of supreme contempt for all other road-users, including, surprisingly, fellow-BMW drivers. However, his lip-curling, nose-wrinkling, head-tossing, finger-snapping, double-parking manner evaporates the second he steps into his wife's Golf when his own car is at the garage. He would love to let other drivers know that the Golf REALLY ISN'T HIS CAR and HE ACTUALLY DRIVES A BMW. Putting a sticker in the window had crossed his mind, but he later realized that it wouldn't necessarily be taken seriously. Poor Michael has the same identity crisis each time he has to hire a car that is not a BMW on one of his many trips abroad. It is like forcing McEnroe to play ping-pong at the youth club.

He edges into lines of traffic with a devastating combination of withering looks and simple thrust. Marina Man and mild-mannered Metro-gnome usually relent and allow him in, as it would appear childish not to; not that they are ever thanked for their troubles. Even Cortina Man, who normally NEVER lets anyone in, reluctantly moves over. Builders' vans are something that he would never attempt to take on, along with taxis, buses and other BMWs, and he would NEVER let a Fuego by.

TRIUMPH TR7

Playboy of the Western Avenue

Although Kevin has a *Playboy* bunny motif on the back of his British Racing Green car, he is an avid reader of *Mayfair* magazine. It is not the articles on steam trains, vintage cars or second world war aeroplanes that interest him; he is obsessed with GIRLS. He thinks about them virtually all the time. He spends most of his day at the office fantasizing about doing something unspeakable behind the filing cabinets to young Judy from accounts, or big Barbara from reception. Or, better still, both together. He dreams of taking Jackie, the boss's secretary, out to an expensive and exclusive night-club, and then back to his 'bachelor pad' in his nippy little sports car for a night of torrid love on his water-bed. The nearest he has got to fulfilling his dream was a peck on the cheek at the office party.

He felt his sophisticated man-about-town, man-of-the-world image could only be enhanced by the acquisition of a Sports Car, and this in turn would help him to 'pull the birds'. He did have some modest success, particularly with the school-leavers in the typing pool, but he was usually thwarted by the fast-talking reps with their *Cortinas*, of all things. And John in Export does alright and he's only got an *Escort*. And Brian in Design certainly does alright, and HE DOESN'T DRIVE AT ALL.

FIAT PANDA

Debbie thinks all cars should have a gender and a pet-name. As soon as she took delivery of this, her first car, she christened *Her* 'Chi-Chi'. She also stuck a Snoopy in Flying Helmet on the back, and a sign reading MY OTHER CAR IS A PORSCHE in the rear window. For a short time, she had a Snoopy hanging from the rear-view mirror, until her older brother, Charles, told her it was considered 'naff'.

Debbie works as a PA/secretary to the MD of a property company. She shares a flat in Fulham (3rd Female, tidy and humorous, to share spacious flat, non-smoker, own room, £35pw). Debbie's delight is being able to drive herself to and from parties, without relying on young chaps' offers of a lift home, which invariably involves unwanted complications. The trouble now is that, being the only one with a car, she ends up ferrying her flat-mates around. Lucinda, a sometime chalet-girl, has a boyfriend with an MGB, but they are always quarrelling and so he isn't always around; she wobbles about on an ancient Raleigh with a basket, listening to Dire Straits on her Sony Walkman. Philippa is also a fair-weather cyclist, although she prefers Linda Ronstadt. Any one of these girls would be **absolutely horrified** if she were described as a Sloane Ranger. **Heaven forbid.** Whatever next?

Turin' Car

18

VW BEETLE

Prole Position

Gary is a bearded *Tribune*-reading social-worker living and working in the Peoples' Republic of Haringey. He drives an orange Beetle with a colour co-ordinated YNNI NIWCLIAR? – DIM DIOLCH sticker on the back. He is 'into' the Chi Kung Science for Internal and Central Energy Movement for Health and Self Defence, which he finds *extremely* 'supportive'. He managed to remain a student until the age of twenty-nine, when he ran out of post-graduate courses, and council grants. He met his girlfriend Mandy, a teacher, through an ad he answered in *Time Out*: 'Sensitive, attractive, slim, Gemini graduate, interests peace, music, macramé, seeks similar far out guy for together times.'

Gary has never put the amphibious properties of his water beetle to the test; he knows it is hermetically sealed, and opening a window when closing the door has become second nature – no more popping ears for him. Also, opening a door on a hot summer day produces the same warm puff got from unscrewing a hot-water bottle. In spite of the all-round weather-proof qualities of his everlasting car, Gary wears a woolly hat and khaki Parka all the year round. True to the advertisements, his car has never broken down, although it has never been serviced in the eight years he has owned it.

Apart from DIY acupuncture, Gary's other hobbies include banning the bomb, boycotting Barclays and stopping the bloody whaling.

MINI COUNTRYMAN

OAP651M

Traveller with My Aunt

When not making green tomato chutney for the WI, Madge and Betty set off for the day in Madge's ten-year old mini with their sheepskin coats, headscarves, tweed skirts and thermos, tupperware and tartan travelling rug. In the back sits Dipper, her even older labrador (the colour of Betty's nicotined fingers). Smoking is not allowed in the car and it's years since they had a row about it. Madge does all the driving while Betty prepares the picnic lunch, and they both share the petrol. Both lost their husbands, one to a land-mine in Malaya and the other to a blond secretary called Gloria. Neither re-married.

They spend a lot of time in the Cotswolds visiting National Trust properties (they are both One in a Million), stately homes, RHS gardens and, best of all, country house sales. They never actually buy anything, but they like to guess how much each item will fetch. The flatulent old dog waits patiently in the car, with the windows open, while Madge and Betty discuss the day's furniture and pictures over cream teas and souvenir catalogues in a tea-room in Stow-on-the-Wold or Bourton-on-the-Water.

Madge does not believe in taking risks and has never had an accident, although she has probably caused dozens. She drives cautiously and very rarely overtakes. The long queue of frustrated drivers on the Traveller's tail overtake when they can, and sometimes when they can't; this underlines Madge's belief that overtaking is a dangerous manoeuvre undertaken by lunatics.

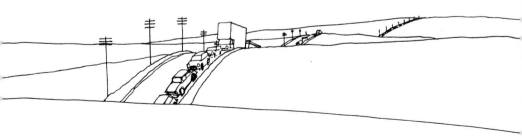

MORGAN PLUS 8

Topless à Go-go

Mild-mannered, bespectacled, white-coated research chemist, Roger, transmutes at weekends into mild-mannered, bespectacled, tweed-jacketed Outdoorsman. When it is merely drizzling, he leaves the hood down and dons a puffy blue anorak which, at speed, inflates to Bibendum proportions, and flaps like a wind-sock in a gale; a sort of anoraks nervoşa. With a half-chewed Briar clenched firmly in his teeth, and his steely-blue eyes fixed firmly on the middle distance, he heads for the hills.

'Girlfriends? Never had much time for them m'self. Always whining on about something or other. Too cold . . . too wet . . . too draughty . . . too bumpy . . . hungry . . . tired . . . want to spend a penny . . . there's always something to moan about. Miserable creatures. 'Cept Daphne. She was a good sort. Went off to Canada, though, to become a lumberjill, or somesuch. The rest of them you can forget. Last one – works at the lab – didn't even know what a dip-stick was. Thought it was something quite different. I ask you. Well, she had to go.'

Roger is an avid rock-climber and loves nothing more than going off to the Welsh mountains and spending a weekend under canvas. It reminds him of his youth in the scouts and his time in the school cadets. It also reminds him of his Morgan with the hood up. He regards saloon-car drivers in shirtsleeves, with the heating on full blast and the windows up, as wets in perambulators, with AA nannies to change their fan-belts.

RENAULT 20TX

Just as the Lancia fancier has a love-affair with anything Italian, so the Renault owner is a complete Francophile. Max not only likes truffles and Truffaut, he smokes Gauloises, drinks Pernod, eats frogs' legs and snails – and you should see escargot! His car is the latest of a long succession of French cars since he first drove around in a red corrugated 2CV as a student, known as the van rouge.

Some critics maintain that French cars are either *too* functional, like the 4L, or they are *over*-designed, like the Citroën GS, with its baffling pair of 'switch-pod' modules, which require the skills of an accordian-player rather that those of a driver. Max writes these people off as the same Philistines who think the Pompidou Centre looks like an oil-refinery.

Max has adopted 'le style Français', which involves driving to work too fast, too close and too loose. He speeds through his own circuituous route of suburban back-doubles one-handed (adroitly à la main gauche, or gauchely à la main droite), that he has evolved through years of commuting.

Some French cars ave rear-wheel drive...
...and some avant.

French without Gears

LAND ROVER

Country Cousin

Up hill, down dale, up dale, down hill, day in, day out, year in year out, in all weathers, till the cows come home. Only once has Albert's work-horse let him down on the precipitous sheep-run (also known as Albert's ewe-turn), and that was when the carburettor filled with mud. It has never been cleaned, never seen the inside of a car-wash, or felt the soft caress of a chamois. In winter it gets sand-blasted by the nor'-easters that whistle across the moors, and in summer the mud dries and falls off in chunks going across cattle-grids.

Albert once went courting a lass in the next valley, but as his only passengers up till then had been sheepdogs, sheep and the vet, the relationship did not develop beyond that first evening. He has been approached on market day by slick young car-salesmen extolling the virtues of the Subaru 4-wheel-drive estate, but to him, if getting himself a wife meant driving around in some limp-wristed saloon-car, then he would rather remain a one-car bachelor.

Down on Animal Farm they have a saying: 'Four-wheel-drive good, two-wheel-drive bad,' and although all cars are equal, some are more equal than others.

PORSCHE 911 TURBO

Rich man, Porsche man

Paul is still a little embarrassed at having a car which he has not yet mastered. Le (real) Man's car *demands* to be driven at 150 mph down the Mulsanne straight, and only fractionally less down the King's Road. Although he hasn't quite got the hang of driving as fast as it *should* be driven, he feels he is *expected* to burn rubber at every opportunity, for the benefit of the hordes of attending spectators he feels *sure* are watching. This may explain why he never looks anywhere except straight ahead.

If, as they say, you can tell a man by the company car he keeps, then Paul should be fast, flash, expensive and brutishly handsome. To him, this is the zenith of company carmanship. The ultimate adman's motor. It would seem that the only people who drive Porsche Turbos are the admen who created a world for themselves to live in, which is peopled by young trendies in Porsche Turbos. They are meant to ski with effortless ease, windsurf, sail, glide, fly, drink Martini, smoke Marlboro, shave with Braun, aftershave with Givenchy. In reality, they drink lager, don't smoke and save with the Halifax, and Paul wouldn't say turBo to a goose.

VW MICROBUS

Gus and Bronwen have always had a nomadic streak. They met on an overland hippie trip to Nirvana in the sixties, when he was trying to return to his native Australia. He was driving an orange VW bus then with 'Sydney or Bust' and kangaroos painted on the side. After he made Sydney without being busted, he came back to Britain, where he sold the bus outside Australia House for what he paid to some other disillusioned Aussies, and moved in with Bron. Twenty years on, and they still have a trace of wanderlust.

He is a gardener, and she a teacher, and her long school-holidays, and Gus being his own boss, mean that they can take off at any time throughout the summer. They tend to gravitate towards folk festivals, and having the Microbus (a shiny, new beige one) allows them to stay in it wherever they choose to stop. Late at night, high on a hill-side in Merioneth, the nasal strains of 'No, nay, never; no, nay, never no more...' can be heard above the lambing sheep. Earth-mother of two teenage children, Bronwen still has an affection for loose-fitting Indian smocks, Peruvian ponchos, long corduroy skirts and desert boots. Gus has a beard, and wears outsize dungarees, a checked lumberjack shirt, and sandals. They both wear glasses, and he smokes roll-ups.

MUS 1C

Volks-singers

RANGE ROVER

Sloane Rangerover

The *urban* version of the Range Rover is a pure statement of vehicular tautology: why have two-wheel drive where four will do? After all, the roads from Wardour Street to Hampstead are perilously steep. The closest this car gets to the country is the grass verge outside the Spaniards Inn on Sunday mornings.

Derek works for a film production company and he once took his new Sloane Rangerover to a shoot in the Cotswolds (film rather than pheasant), but the car became so dirty that the exercise was never repeated. To look at Derek's five day growth of beard, black leather bomber-jacket and white baseball boots, one could be forgiven for thinking that appearances couldn't matter a jot, but how confusing it all is; the bomber jacket, so casually slung over his shoulders à la James Dean, cost him over £300 in South Molton Street, and the early David Putnam beard takes him longer to perfect each day than it would to shave.

A number of Sloane Rangerovers actually come up to town from places as far afield as Weybridge, Godalming and Virginia Water. Londoners stand open-mouthed in amazement as they watch these powerful machines perform feats of acrobatic prowess and rugged athleticism, like mounting kerb-stones with ease, and carrying the weekly Sainsbury shop with seemingly no effort at all.

The *proper* Rustic Rover, on the other hand, is frequently found in muddy fields; after all, it was designed with that in mind. Although most of the muddy fields are at race-meetings, school open-days, hunter-trials, and agricultural shows, the 4-wheel-drive comes into its own, running rings round Volvos and Mercedes-Benz. Some Range Rovers have been spotted in Real Country, however, mostly on grouse-moors, but sightings are rare.

The Range Rover is as indispensible as green wellies and matching huskies, particularly in Wiltshire, Gloucester and Hampshire. Since the car received the Royal seal of approval (to say nothing of Papal), it has become a great favourite amongst both loyalists and Catholics alike.

Although they very rarely get involved in anything agricultural, some are believed to have carried the odd bale of hay or sack of pony-feed. The tail-gate, when lowered, however, turns the car into an ideal four-door saloon-bar. Bar-stools are optional extras.

RENAULT 4

The Renault 4 is the nearest Peter can get to the pretence that he is not really driving a car at all. A number of reasons, the lack of public transport being the most persuasive, have forced him, reluctantly, to take to the road. In some respects he pretends he is riding a bicycle rather than a smelly, anti-social death-trap, belching out noxious, toxic fumes. He regards the motorcar as a necessary evil, and hates the idea of being included in the generic term 'motorist'; the very word holds the same loathing to him as 'nuclear fall-out' and 'estate agent'.

Peter is a lecturer at the poly and his duffle-coat, desert boots, red knitted tie and dark shirt are a legacy of his days at Reading University reading history in the sixties. The shapeless brown corduroy jacket is in fact new and the latest in a long line going back twenty years. His glasses are strongly influenced by Dave Brubeck, whose music he still plays, along with Gerry Mulligan and Charlie Parker. Not a lot has changed for Peter since he used to have philosophical discussions about Wittgenstein and Sartre over a mug of cocoa in his Redbrick days; although he has seen change and decay all around him, there have been a few advances, notably real-ale, bottle-banks and the *Guardian* being printed in London.

Van Ordinaire

FERRARI 308GTB

Pasta Performance

Mimo is gift-wrapped for the gossip columnists. He is young, rich, and goes to, and more importantly, is seen at, all the right places: Monaco for the Grand Prix, Longchamps for the Arc de Triomphe. Cowdray Park for the polo, and Gstaad for the backgammon. He is one of an endangered species: the playboy. He doesn't work as such; he dabbles. His enormous inheritance has made him prey to a horde of very much unendangered females of the species. Not that he feels in the slightest bit victimized; a Ferrari without a vacuous blonde is like a Morris Marina without a nodding dog in the rear window.

He looks as though he has been invented by an advertising agency to promote aftershave. He wears electric-blue shirts, dark blue cashmere blazer, beige trousers and white Gucci slip-ons. After the car has whined past, the air is pervaded by an overwhelming odour of Paco Rabanne, which almost smothers the exhaust fumes. His dark hair is slicked back and gently laps over his collar, and his perennial sun-tan has the highly-polished, well-buffed look of an amber ornament.

Mimo is a good, fast driver, and does not get drawn into dices with lesser mortals in lesser motors, unlike Porsche Man, who can resist nothing. Mimo *knows* he can beat almost anything on the road. Except Porsches. Anyone else who overtakes the Ferrari driver only does so with *his* permission.

SAAB TURBO

Bjorn to Lead

This is The Caar for Robert, the young-ish middle-management executive (note black leather 'executive' attaché case), with a young-ish wife, Carol (known as Mem-saab), and a young family (note baby-seat for two-year-old Jason and part of toy that infuriatingly rolls around on the parcel-shelf when cornering). He takes his driving seriously (black leather 'driving' gloves and *AA Book of the Road*), tries to stave off the inevitable and encircling spread from too many expensive-account lunches in and around Charlotte Street (squash racket on rear shelf), still follows motor racing trends (copy of *Motor Sport* on back seat and straight-arm driving technique). He used to have an MGB but was forced to change it for 'something more sensible, if we are going to start a family'. The Saab was the perfect choice; it was only when they were bowling along at over 110 mph that Carol realized it was much quicker that the 'sporty' MGB. Gone are his carefree 'roof down and foot down' days, but he still manages to scrape up a modicum of pleasure from his daily journey to and from work, and he still sometimes reflects that maybe he should have taken up rallying professionally when he had the chance.

MINI METRO

Mr Norman Normal is a supervisor at the Department of Stealth and Total Obscurity. He has worked there for twenty-three years. Nothing ever takes Norman by surprise. His life is far too planned to cater for surprises. Norman is a Metrognome. His day is planned down to the last detail. He allows a five-minute tolerance from the time he reverses the Metro out of the car-port and into Acacia Drive, to the moment he parks in his designated space at the Department. He *never* varies his route. He leaves work at 5.07 and, with a regulated stop to buy an evening paper, he is home in time to watch the 5.40 News on BBC, before having his tea, which Norma, his wife, has prepared. 'Is that you, Dear?' she calls out from the kitchen, when she hears the front-door key being turned in the lock. It invariably is. It has been for the past twenty-three years.

When he has to fill up with petrol every other week, he sets off five minutes early, and goes to a service station that provides him with exactly that. 'None of this self-service nonsense. After all, we pay enough for the petrol as it is; why shouldn't we get a bit of service?' Every Sunday morning, Norman devotes an hour to prostrating himself before the Chrome Altar. He doth both inside, and out. Being a keen handyman-about-the-house, he is also his own serviceman-about-the-car, and performs tricky open-bonnet surgery on such things as the air filter and tappet adjustment, with the aid of the owner's manual.

Metrognome

MERCEDES BENZ 280TE

German cars have long had a reputation for high-precision engineering. Even Shakespeare, although not a motorist himself, made a passing reference to them in the *Merchant of Venice*.

Shylock: On what compulsion must I? Tell me that.

Porsche: The quality of Mercedes is not Strain'd.

Guy became a two-ton Teuton car man because he wanted the doors to shut with the same metallic clunk as a Braun table lighter or a Mauser automatic. Being a keen sportsman and a 'useful shot' he likes aiming his car through the 3-pointed sights at the end of the long-barrelled bonnet. 'There is something to be said for always having a constant reminder of what car you are driving in your view,

Estate Car Name

whichever way you turn.' The dogs all wear ID discs with two addresses, one town, the other country. On Friday evening Guy's striped shirt is changed for a beige roll-necked sweater, hacking jacket with leather patches, and cords, for the drive to the country. Arabella merely has to adjust her headscarf.

When Guy first bought the Ludwig Van, he was driven nearly round the Benz by his friends clicking their heals, calling him Mein Führer and muttering such things as 'Who von ze var, anyvay?'; 'Slow down! You Goethe Faust'; and 'Look, Fritz, no Hans.' However, he put this down to nothing more than *Saure Weinbeeren*, as his car was not only faster off the mark than their Volvos and Fords, it cost far more, too.

)esire

PONTIAC TRANS AM

Stavros has interests in coin-op laundrettes, doner-kebab takeaways and girls. He spends a lot of his evenings cruising up and down the Finchley Road, dropping in on his various properties in North London, and, if lucky, picking up Scandinavian au pair girls in wine-bars and night-clubs that cater for the lonely and homesick. The 'Nanny à Gogo' is just such an establishment. His open-necked *crêpe de chine* shirt (open, that is, to the navel) reveals a thick matt-black matted chest in which is entwined a gold medallion the size of a Frisbee. A pair of sun-glasses nestle on the matching thick black curls on his head. He wears a pair of white jeans that are so tight they look as though they have been sprayed on with an aerosol; this is so that Heidi and Gretchen can do a spot of window-shopping or, as he calls it, shopping by male-order.

In the Traffic Lights Grand Prix Stavros intimidates most of the opposition by constantly revving the big V8. On the turns, however, he is an even bigger Prix and loses out to smaller and more agile cars as he trickles round on tiptoe. He doesn't find this at all ego-chipping as he is able to blast past again when the road straightens out. He finds his own performance much more interesting; his motor-carnal knowledge is probably unsurpassed West of the Balkans and North of Kentish Town. There are not many things that Stavros hasn't done in his Ponceac parked by Hampstead Heath on the way to taking Gunilla back to her employer's house in Golders Green.

Macho Machine

FORD CAPRI

Squeals on Wheels

Trev works in the building trade, and was thus able to buy his mo'er for cash, after a particularly good year. He chose a C'pree partly because it fitted in with his Brut aftershave and suède-jacket image; fast cars, fast women, and slow thinkers. And partly because, of all the people in the world, he would like to be Bodie, from the *Professionals*; and *He* drives one, too. Trev is a bit of a lad when it comes to fast-talking the girls. His rum-and-coke, saloon-bar manner soon has Sandra, and her friend, enthralled. 'I'll have a Bacardi and lemonade, and she'll have a Pernod and coke, won't you, Cheryl?' Sandra has a short cony coat and a black bra under her white frilly blouse.

Trev gets a lot of his dialogue from *Minder*, another of his favourites – a case of life imitating art. 'D' you wanna go dahn the frog in the jam-jar to the rub-a-dub for quick Vera or a gold watch, or have you got to get back to her indoors?'† He can hardly wait for the next *Rocky*, and he still believes that Bruce Lee is alive and kicking somewhere in Hong Kong. Trev is concerned about keeping in shape, and every week he goes weight-lifting. When he goes to Majorca or Ibiza (he has never been to C'pree), for his summer holidays, he devotes himself to sunbathing. The tan, the tee-shirt and the C'pree make him pretty well irresistible.

---

†'Do you want to go down the road in the car to the pub for a quick gin or a scotch, or should you return to see your wife at home?'

AUDI 100CD

David tries to keep up with the trends in car design, but technical advances are winging their way in at a bewildering rate. 'A few years ago the rage was all rear spoilers, but look at them now; that Sierra XR4 is a mess. Not one, but TWO rear parcel-shelves. On the OUTSIDE. Then it was front air-dams. Last year everything was TURBO. This year it's all co-efficient of drag. Or DRAG FACTOR, as we like to call it. But you've got to keep up with the fads. Audi have been pretty good on the novelty front; front-wheel drive, FOUR-wheel-drive, four cylinders, FIVE cylinders, fuel injection and now, NO air-dam, NO rear spoilers, and flush-fitting windows, to say nothing of the malfunctions display panel and 'Econ' gauge.'

'I can go back as far as Les Leston wooden-rimmed steering-wheels. Then along came little black leather ones the size of a stop-cock. AND Minilite wheels. Had a set on my Cooper S. No chequered tape, though. And I never really cared for those personalized wind-screen sun-visors, you know the sort of thing: Darren and Sharon, or Dennis and Rodney. I must say, I did think that we'd all be running around in 'ground-effect' skirts this year, but they've been banned in Formula One. I wonder what's next? Wire wheels and knock-off hub-caps?'

Drag Racer

ROLLS-ROYCE

As everybody knows, one needs bread to buy a Rolls. Which model one owns depends on how one acquired one's wealth.

The Aristocracy prefer to be driven in a Silver Spoon, whereas Sammy, a fat little ulcerous record producer feels more at home in the Silver Tongue. Silver Tongue owners occasionally aspire to the rarefied heights of the Silver Spooners, but small details – like the habit of *always* smoking a Davidoff No. 1 in a flamboyant manner, even at eight o'clock in the morning whilst strap-hanging in the back, in such a way as to expose three inches of Harvie and Hudson cuff, lapis–lazuli cuff-links and an 18ct yellow-gold Piaget – give the game away. In the back, at 60mph, the loudest sound he hears is the ticking of his pacemaker.

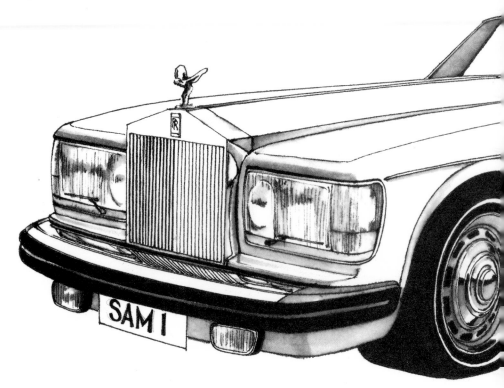

Sammy's Roller-disco, as he calls it, is in fact a few years old, but he very cleverly invested in a personalized number-plate when he bought it new, so it doesn't now show its years. Even *he* thinks they are becoming a trifle common, particularly at Royal Ascot, where they are so many trying to squeeze into the car-parks, what begins as mild congestion can soon develop into jam rolls.

Early English Perpendicular

BENTLEY MULSANNE

Roles Apart

SNO 88Y

Piers is unquestionably as rich as the master of the Rolls, but while appearing to be less ostentatious he is, in fact, masking a social awareness of such subtlety it baffles all but the cognoscenti. He is making a far stronger statement about his taste and discernment, and that, in itself, transcends any accusation of inverted snobbery through that well-tried device – the double-bluff.

He raves about films he sees in New York six months before they reach London, and then finds them 'boring, predictable and over-simplistic' when everyone else has seen them, just as he stops going to restaurants once they are written up in *Vogue* or *Harpers*. As the Bentley represents a fraction of Rolls-Royce production, Piers already scores heavily for rarity value. He carries this dilettantism through to his wardrobe; everything he wears is hand-made. He drinks Louis Roederer Cristal (*never* anything so vulgar as Dom Perignon, or Krug) and Laphroig malt whisky, although that is becoming far too available, and wears Kaffe Fassett knitwear at week ends ('My dear chap, Missoni is simply *too* common'). He chose the silver paintwork as he felt it matched his distingué side-burns.

To call Piers an élitist would be like calling Sheraton a chippy. Although this sort of studied eccentricity is perhaps too abstruse for the Proles–Royce rabble, it is regarded by the purist few who *know* as being too clever by one and a half.

FORD ESCORT XR3i

Barry has a sticker in the rear window which reads, WINDSURFERS DO IT STANDING UP. 'It' can only refer to nose-picking, as he does little else while driving. Social behaviourists and psychologists are baffled as to why there is such a high incidence of this activity in Fords. In a recent survey, Fords came out proportionally higher than any other make, with a staggering 96%; this is 20% higher than the next marque, the Rover, and nearly 28% more than the Audi. The proportion of women-pickers to men is 1 in 5, and rising, with the top car, for the third year running, the Volvo. Saabs and TR7s hardly feature at all, but this can be put down to the fact that most of the drivers are hampered by the wearing of gloves.

Not only does Barry do it standing up on a windsurfer, he is one of a water-skiing syndicate that rents a flooded gravel-pit in Sussex. He met Nicky at an après-water-ski barbeque by the lakeside one balmy summer's evening, and he fell immediately, and deeply, in lust with her. However, what started as a frivolous affair ended in marriage, when Nicky became pregnant; this effectively put an untimely end to Barry's libertine career, and could explain why, when seen together in the car, they are constantly arguing.

Pick-up Truck

ROVER 3500

Dickie usually stops off for a 'quick half' at the Hare and Hounds (known affectionately as the Hair of the Dog) on his way back from his light engineering factory on the trading estate. 'Evening, George. Brr – bit nippy out. Hul-lo, Charlie, long time no see. What's yours? No, no, nonono, I'll get these. G and T was it? Two large ones please, George. And one for yourself. Cheers.' He doesn't remove his sheepskin car coat (also known as a Rovercoat), as he is not staying long. At weekends he sports a blue blazer with silver buttons, cravat, cavalry twills and suède shoes. Dickie always wears suède shoes. 'Well, must dash, the little wife'll be worrying where I am. Well, alright, maybe just one for the road. No, no, nonono, it's my shout. Same again please, George, and one for yourself. Cheers.'

Just as he refers to his wife with the definite article, he uses the third person feminine pronoun for his car. 'She's a good little runner. Will cruise all day at the ton. Never complains. Christ, you see some bloody idiots on the roads though. There was this bloke this evening in a Marina or something. Came out from nowhere right in front of me. Bit of quick thinking on my part, I can tell you. Could have been nasty. Strawberry jam. Bloody idiot, shouldn't be allowed on the bloody roads, if you'll pardon my French'.

After a couple more for the road he heads homeward at high speed. 'I think I actually drive better after a couple of stiff ones.' As usual his dinner is in the oven, and, as usual, the wife is watching television in a room which, with its open beams, horse brasses, hunting prints and leaded windows, looks not unlike the Lounge Bar at the Hair of the Dog.

Roverambitious

MORRIS 1300 ESTATE

The Reverend Baxter McLaren, the vicar of St Jude's, needs a car to visit his parishioners, who are spread like broken fan-belts across the countryside. His stipend does not run to a new car, so he has to rely on a fifteen-year-old Morris he shares with his wife, which is fast going the way of all flesh: earth to earth, ashes to ashes, rust to rust. As a curate (a sort of learner driver) he pedalled round the parish on a lady's Rudge with a basket on the front, and then, for a while, he had a motor scooter, and became known parochially as either a ton-up vicar or a Hell's Anglican, riding his Vespa to matins, although the more unkind element in the village regarded him as a verger on the ridiculous. His first car was a Morris 1000 Tourer, known simply as the Convert, and when he got his own parish and an ample wife, he plumped for something larger, but maintained his marque loyalty.

He conducts two services every Sunday, although his car only gets one every 5000 miles, and he frequently uses Motoring as a theme for his sermons, as it is a subject all his congregation understands. 'Dearly beloved, I have chosen for today's text 2 Kings ix, 9, "The Driving is like the driving of Jehu, the son of Nimshi, for he driveth furiously" . . . *For he driveth furiously.* Y'know, we are all of us on the motorway of Life. Some of us are "driving furiously" in the fast lane. Others are tootling along, quite happily, in the slow lane, getting to where we are going, nonetheless. I sometimes feel I am on the hard shoulder, with a flat tyre, and a broken rev counter. Do you ever feel like that? Well, don't despair. The Lord, in the shape of the RAC man, will soon be along in his little blue van to patch things up and send you on your way. I am not the RAC man. If you like, I am your Minister of Transport, your lay-by priest, who can tell you where to go, and how to get there . . .

And now, let us sing "All things bright and beautiful", paying special attention to the second verse:

> The rich man in his castle
> The poor man at his gate
> God made them high or lowly
> And order'd their estate.'

And if his prayers are answered, he would dearly love a Volvo, although he would accept a Ford. Or a Citroën. In fact anything that was less than three years old and capacious enough to drive them all out of the temple and down to the seaside.

Revving-up

VW GOLF GTI

Agent Estate

Known in the US as the 'Rabbit' (or 'Hutchback'), this model has been multiplying at such a rate in the past few years it has reached epidemic proportions. Nigel bought his when in the army on the Rhine, and found that simply owning one was enough to qualify him as an estate agent when he returned to civvie street. He drives with great speed around town, and on the motorway to and from his parents' house in Wiltshire at weekends. He likes seeing his parents each week, and besides, it's a very convenient way to get his laundry done in time for Sunday evening.

Because of his tall good-looks and undemanding intellect he is very popular with the parents of good-looking intellectually undemanding young things, and is consequently highly sought after at weekends. In town, he shares a flat off the Brompton Road with three other chaps (two estate agents and an articled solicitor), and they have worked out a rota system for entertaining these young things. Although Nigel's culinary expertise is limited to spaghetti Bolognese (from a tin) and scrambled eggs, after a few well-chosen and persuasive words to Mummy, his candle-lit tête-à-têtes often feature delicious steak and kidney pies and beef strogonof – another very good reason for going home.

Nigel has an extensive collection of headgear on the back window shelf to cater for every eventuality – flat cap, deerstalker, trilby, fedora – he can always be relied upon to produce a hat out of the Rabbit.

JEEP RENEGADE

Four-wheel drivel

Bob could hardly be described as a renegade himself – he has been faithful to the Beach Boys for nearly twenty years. He first went to the West Coast for a month when he left art college. This was just after David Hockney had made a splash or two out there. Bob was immediately seduced by the sun, sea, surf, sand and sex-life-style of California. He peroxided his hair, sawed off his jeans and slipped on a pair of white baseball boots.

Now in his early forties, he still hankers after the Californian dream. He still goes to the West Coast, this time on business; the girls seem to get younger and have moved on to roller-skates, where he can't follow, except with his eyes. Partly to re-capture the Good Vibrations, and partly to stay young, he bought a Jeep with four on the floor. The trouble is that the Great West Road *isn't* the Pacific Coast Highway 101, and surfing in Cornwall in the pouring rain isn't *quite* the same as hanging ten on Malibu. However, there are a few sunny days when he can turn down the hood, turn up *Little Deuce Coupe,* turn off the main road and turn on; and, with a lemon-haired lady in a tee-shirt, a can of Schlitz, and his eyes shut, he is *almost* there.

CITROËN GS

John and Jo both work in design, she in fashion, he in graphics. They made the transpontine move to Clapham years before it was remotely considered fashionable. Being ahead of one's time does have its drawbacks; apart from bricks through the windows in the early days, their house is a curious mixture of style and fashions. They stopped shopping at Habitat when Terence Conran discovered high-Tech, but they still have a legacy of stripped pine, Blue Denmark china and red

The Hatchback of Notre Dame

plastic Crayonne bathroom accessories. Their kitchen looks like a fifties coffee bar in rural Wales, with wire chairs and orange PVC tablecloth, and the knocked-through sitting/dining room like Gamages before the war, with display cases filled with Dinky toys and tin cars.

John vacillates sartorially between oversized American hand-me-downs with skinny ties and dog-eared collars, and bomber lumber-jackets, white plastic Flip sunglasses and white Kickers. Jo wears almost anything that girls fifteen years her junior have thrown together. They share the car, she dropping him off in Covent Garden on her way to Camden Town and picking him up again in the evening. Once a week they stay up in town to see a movie, (something Latvian at the ICA), or a rock concert, preferably New Wave.

At weekends they load the car up to capacity with house and garden tools, and drive to their converted chapel in Suffolk. They take their two cats with them, and they roam about the car free-range, with Genghis on the back window shelf, and Immanuel Kant (the neutered tom) alternating between John's shoulder and a position under the brake pedal. Before the cats, Jo had a parrot, which used to sit on the head-rest. John christened it the Flying Car-pet.

DAIMLER SOVEREIGN

Contrary to popular belief, Len acquired his camel-hair coat long before buying the Daimler. Only the bookie's hat and membership of the golf-club came afterwards. He owns the local garage and was able to get the club secretary a very favourable deal on his new Austin Ambassador. Len served an apprenticeship in the early fifties at the Warren Street College of Automotive Studies, and consequently knows a few back-doubles when it comes to the motor trade. Len enjoys a round of golf of a Sunday morning before his roast dinner, and he has become famous for his seemingly endless fount of risqué jokes over a drinkie at the nineteenth hole.

With the boys grown up and having flown the neo-Georgian nest, Len and Sylvia are able to get out for a meal of a Saturday night with another couple. He doesn't feel its been a proper evening out unless his steak has been flambéed à table, and the Châteauneuf du Pape presented in a wine-basket, and the Liebfraumilch in an ice–bucket, so they tend to go to the Country Club. Sylvia is much more adventurous; although she *always* starts with a prawn cocktail, she likes to try dishes like canard à l'orange and pollo supremo with her usual sautée potatoes and courgettes.

Len has been called an 'aggressive' driver by Sylvia. Len resents this, as he is probably one of the most experienced drivers on the road. After all, he used to race Ford Zodiacs and Austin A40s at Snetterton and the like. He does tend to get a little short-tempered with anyone doing less than ninety in the outside lane, although he is very reluctant to be overtaken himself, and puts up a brave fight. He very rarely loses, and he has been known to drive miles out of his way to prove to some ignorant motorist that he can still out-drive anyone, even a young lout in a Lotus.

FLA 5H

From Jags to Riches

BENTLEY 4½ LITRE

Bertie found his mouldering Bentley in a barn, at a time when it was still possible to find a Stutz in a stable or an Alvis in the attic. He lives in a time-warp from fifty years ago, and his clothes echo a bygone age; he positively *bristles* with hounds-tooth tweeds and handle-bar moustache, and the deerstalker, brown brogues and Viyella shirt complete the picture of this rare vintage type. He restored the car himself, and is a frequent entrant at Bentley Drivers Club and VSCC rallies. He also trots along to the 'Noggin and a Natter' evenings (with slide show), held in a room upstairs at the local in rural Sussex.

Along with the other rally-jacketed, deer-stalking, pipe-smoking members, Bertie maintains that no motor car built after 1955 is worth considering. The last *real* sports car was the XK120, although when it came out he thought it had rather a white-walled wide-boy image.

'30 Vintage Sport

'Of course you can't take the old girl up to town with all those noddies trying to smash their Morris Marinas into you, can you? Although I dare say their little tin boxes wouldn't stand a chance against a motor car that was built to last. They knew how to build motor cars in those days.'

Alfapseud

Julia runs her own interior design company. And a house. And two children. And a nanny. And an ex-husband. And a car. Occasionally she has to borrow Maurice's estate to pick up a piece of furniture. 'It's all *frightfully* civilised. Very Iris Murdoch, I know, but we *are* grown-ups.' The only problem is that HER car comes back reeking of cigarette smoke and Rive Gauche, like an errant husband with lip-stick on his collar – and Maurice didn't even SMOKE. This was happening before, and was instrumental in, their divorce. His secretary was cited as car-respondent, and it was proved conclusively in court that it *was* possible in an Alfa and that lay-bys were aptly named. The judge said that it brought a whole new meaning to such words as 'auto-eroticism' and 'double de-clutching', and he summed it up as a case of 'driving licentious'.

Julia likes to think of herself as the modern independent career-woman, but is by no means a women's libber. She enjoys being tooted at by lorry-drivers, and would welcome the appearance of a Lothario-in-a-Lancia or a Romeo in another Alfa, to change a wheel in a downpour, even though she is perfectly capable of changing it herself. Maurice used to tell her she drove like a man. She was offended only because she reckoned she drove better than a man. She thinks he drives like an old woman most of the time, with occasional flashes of Attila the Hun and, when unduly provoked, Nemesis.

LINCOLN CONTINENTAL

The Family Car

Dino is a Family man and, as he has such a large Family, (mostly godchildren), he needs a large Family limo. He is a nocturnal predator, and shuns daylight; most things about him are to do with shade – his sun-glasses, the tinted windows on his car, his business. His night-time activities involve touring around the West End and making collections from his many interests; video hire shops, gambling clubs, bars and amusement arcades. He is driven everywhere by an eighteen-stone

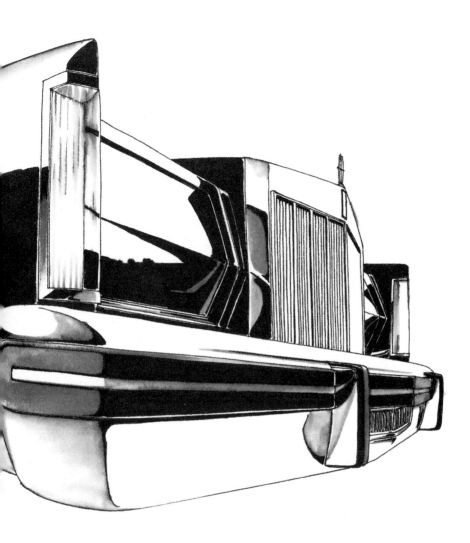

minder called Victor, who wears an ill-fitting suit of a shiny blue material. Dino has never actually driven the car himself. In fact, he doesn't possess a driving licence.

He is also something of a film producer and has been known to conduct auditions in the deep-pile wall-to-wall luxury of the back seat, whilst being driven around the Outer Circle of Regent's Park. Any young hopeful who can hold his interest for more than three laps at a constant 25mph is in with a chance of appearing in one of his 'art' movies. This kind of practical examination is also known as the 'Continental Congress'.

MERCEDES BENZ 500SEC

Des was infuriated at first when he spotted a sticker in the back of a Ford Fiesta bearing the message: 'This car may not be fast, but it's paid for, and it's in front of you.' It didn't stay in front for very long (Des blasted past with his usual sledgehammer subtlety), but a nagging thought remained: it had never ocurred to him that *anyone* might think that *his* car was not paid for. It wasn't. It was leased. Only an arrested cretin would want to spend £30,000 of his *own* money on a car, but as MD of the family furniture business, he wanted others to think that he was rich enough to splash out on something so frivolous as a car if he wanted to.

He began to look around at other cars on the road. He always knew that fleets of company Cortinas with coat-hangers were driven by salesmen in ladies' underwear, and indeed, he had his own flotilla of Ford Sierras with sample swatches on the back seat for his reps, but he never really stopped to think about other luxury executive expresses. Sitting at the lights, Des muses about how many of the people around him own their cars. 'Has anyone ever gone out and actually bought a Merc, or a BMW 7 Series, as a private punter, apart from Middle Eastern businessmen? *He* certainly didn't, that slob in the Roller. And that Romeo in the Alfa, *he* didn't. And what about all those Rovermen? and that fat bookie in the Opel? How many of them *bought* their cars? In fact, has anyone *ever* bought *any* car?'

Coupé de Grâce

HILLMAN MINX

Banger and Smash

George always wears a hat when driving. As does Doris, when sitting beside him. So does the Welsh doll that hangs from the rear-view mirror. They are all off on one of the Hillman's half-dozen outings a year. For the rest of the time, the car is garaged, and gets a pre-journey polish the day before. This is followed by an extensive road-test to the corner shop, and back. 'It's alright, Mother, she's going like a bird.' They have owned the car since new, and if it was ever advertised for sale, it would be one of the few occasions when the statement, 'exceptionally low mileage, one careful owner,' would be true. In fact, it has only done 5,000 miles since new, necessitating, according to the manual, only one service. Hard to believe – although not to the thousands of motorists on the same winding stretch of road half a dozen times a year – the car has never been over 45mph. Unlike his politics, which are staunch Tory, George is very much middle-of-the-road.

They stick to the main roads like snails, as they are patrolled by the boys in yellow. The dark and oily world under the bonnet is a complete mystery to George, and he is always very impressed by the patrolman's skill and knowledge when called out to change a fan-belt, which has simply rotted away, or a top-hose, which has become too tired to hold water. While the change is taking place, George and Doris erect the picnic table and sit in the lay-by, having a nice cup of tea, and watch the traffic thundering past.

ASTON MARTIN

Bernie believes that everyone is looking at him wherever he drives his Social 'Vantage. This is essential to his ego. A bad day at the office is immediately transformed into a good day, by slipping into his car and giving it, as he says 'plenty of wellie'. This has nothing to do with his stature, or the fact that he is in the blue denim side of the rag-trade, or that he has been called a social mountaineer, a *parvenu* (he had to look that one up before he could take offence), and an *arriviste*. He may have been *nouveau pauvre once*, but that was a long time ago; he has managed to cover his tracks quite well, by buying a large house in the country, changing his accent from Whitechapel to neo-Georgian, and *not* marrying the boss's daughter.

Instead, he married the girl-next-door, and Sue has been nurturing, buffing and generally 'improving' him; he still manages to embarrass her, however, with occasional references to 'serviettes', 'toilets' and 'settees'. Bernie has been encouraged to ride, play bridge, learn to play tennis, and show an interest in the theatre, music, and books; Amanda has so far managed to wean him off Harold Robbins, and on to Dick Francis and Jeffrey Archer, but apart from one success with *Guys and Dolls*, he would prefer to 'work late' and meet them afterwards for a meal, rather than sit through three hours of tedium without being able to smoke.

The Social 'Vantage

VAUXHALL CHEVETTE

When Dave and Sharon first set off on Bank Holiday Monday, with Scott, Tracey and Gran in the back, their hopes are set on a sunny day, a trouble-free drive, sandcastles, tea, beer and skittles. Dave is resolved to remain calm and good-natured, whatever happens, but his personal temperature gauge rises dangerously high when they have to return home for the *second* time; the first was because Sharon thought she had left the oven on, and the second was when Gran announced, ten miles out, that she *may* have left a tap running. She hadn't, but this did not prevent an incident which effectively alienated Dave from both his wife and his mother-in-law for most of the outward journey. All communication between Dave and Gran and Dave and Sharon was conducted through Tracey. He even refused to stop to let Gran 'go' until she threatened to 'go' on the Draylon velvet seat-covers.

Vaux Pop

The rear window shows evidence of past sorties; they have seen the lions of Longleat, the dolphins at Windsor, and have watched the monkeys at Woburn wrench out the radio aerial by its roots. This has since been replaced by a bent coat-hanger, known as the Sketchley Special.

After a tortuous drive they spend what remains of the day on the beach. The sand gets everywhere. 'That's why they're called SANDwiches,' quips Gran, as she has done every time they have gone to the seaside. All too soon they are packing up the car and heading home, joining the long line of brake-lights. Apart from Scott, who has thrown up, they all agree they've had a wonderful time and can't wait for the next day out.

OPEL SENATOR

Les is a tax-consultant who can turn an evasion into an avoidance over an expense-account blow-out at the Connaught. He specializes in 'taxtiles', as he likes to call his exiled pop stars, film actors, good old boys who made too much, too soon, on a property deal, and speculators who want to 'lose' a few hundred G's. Every man is an island to Les, and every island is a Man, or a Cayman, or a Guernsey, or a Jersey. He makes his money by saving richer people theirs.

Although he spends his time helping the rich get richer by getting their money *out* of Britain, he professes to be fervently *British*, to the point of jingoism. He easily defends buying a *German* car by saying, 'After all, it's only a Vauxhall with a German accent.' The fact that its parents are American has either never occurred to him, or he doesn't want to know.

He is in a perpetually foul mood, particularly when driving. Whether he is on his way to work after a fierce row with his *incompetent* wife, or on his way home after a fierce row with his *incompetent* secretary, he is not to be tangled with. He is possibly one of the most unpleasant and mannerless of drivers; slumped in his seat, with one hand holding a chewed cigar, and the other firmly on the Horn of Plenty, he is definitely the man to evade (or, rather, avoid).

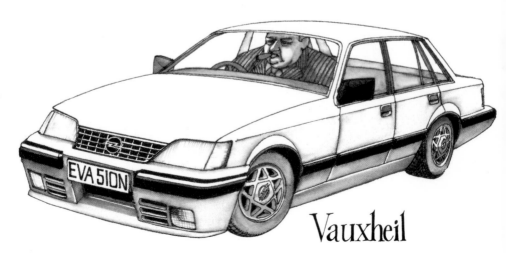

EVA 5ION

Vauxheil

JAGUAR XJS

Marque of the Beast

Although Cyril has retired from the theatrical profession, he is still a familiar face to millions of viewers who have seen him in old 'Sunday afternoon' films and the occasional pro-celebrity golf tournament. He always looks as though he is about to set sail on a boat; deck shoes, denim cap perched jauntily on silver-grey curls, pale Daks slacks, Arnold Palmer homely cashmere cardy, thin silver moustache. He spends a lot of time with Shirley at their apartment in Marbella, and, like her has a hardy perennial tan. The nautical look is not altogether out of place, since he owns a forty-foot cruiser, which is berthed in Lymington Marina.

They often drive down on a Friday night for a weekend's 'pottering about'. Not that he potters about on the road. He is frequently pulled up for speeding, but usually manages to silver-tongue his way out. The Old Bill is invariably charmed by the lovable rogue's performance and is soon eating out of his hand. 'Didn't I see you on the box the other day, sir? . . . well, I'd take it a bit easier if I were you, sir . . . I couldn't have your autograph, could I, sir, it's for my little girl . . .'

They very rarely take the boat out, however; most of the 'pottering about' involves polishing brass and polishing off copious amounts of pink gin. Almost everything on board revolves around drink. The timing of the first one of the day is critical – when does a 'sharpener' become a 'snorter', and at what hour does a 'jigger' become a 'snifter'? After that has been sorted out, with no startling conclusions, the rest of the day's nips, noggins, tots, sundowners, tinctures, libations, potations, and merest toothfuls are plain sailing in comparison. 'Quick ones' are only ever had at the yacht club.

PORSCHE 924

When Babs steps out of her cherry-red Porsche, she is a walking poster-site; she is *heavily* into Logo-Fashion; all her clothes and accessories, save the Alaskan lynx, have the maker's label on the *outside*, legible at up to ten yards. From a large gold 'G'-buckled belt to the Givenchy head-scarf tied casually round the Yves Saint Laurent bag. Although with her figure she ought to be wearing Orson Welles designer-jeans, she has somehow managed to shoehorn herself into Gloria Vanderbildt's. Years of exposure to the Spanish sun and the Swedish sun-bed have turned her skin the colour, and texture, of one of her Gucci handbags.

Logomotion

She is on one of her frequent forays into town from their mini-South Fork-style house in Weybridge, to add to her collection of heavy-gauge Kutchinsky jewellery, and to purchase (she never *buys*) a Sherle Wagner green onyx and gold basin set. Then its time for lunch at Meridiana's with her best friend, Miriam, who has travelled all the way down from St John's Wood, where they discuss diets, health-farms and money. Twice a year they both spend a week, and a great deal of their husband's money, being pummelled, pampered and packed in mud, but then that's what being a Porsche little rich girl is all about.

She wears a Yorkshire terrier under her arm, like a spare handbag, and still props sun-glasses (Porsche, of course) on top of her head, even though Miriam told her they stopped doing that in the South of France years ago. 'I saw a picture of Barbara Streisand the other day with *her* glasses on top of *her* head, and you wouldn't call *her* passée, would you?' Both Babs and her husband, Sidney, have always been 'liberal thinkers' when it came to sex, and come it did a few years ago at a party in neighbouring Esher. When she was obliged to toss her car-keys into a fruit bowl, Babs was more concerned about someone else driving her car; however, once she realized that no one was particularly interested in driving she soon got the hang of it and has never looked back.

LANCIA COUPÉ

In the Spring a young man's Lancia lightly turns off the road and heads for the woods, with thoughts of love. Jonathan is too grown-up for that sort of thing, but he is still a Lancia-fancier and has been having a love-affair with Roman romanticism for ages. He acquired a Lancia not just because he could not afford a Ferrari, but because he has long held the belief that anything Italian is stylish, racy, and a touch macho.

He spends summer holidays in a Tuscan farmhouse. He spends money in Italian restaurants. He orders in Italian and he finds it as impossible *not* to speak menu-Italian as he does *not* twisting his hands round and round when asking for the pepper-mill. He wears Cerutti, Missoni, Armani and Gucci; in fact, he wears anything that ends in an 'i'. His house is mélange of minimal Magistretti furniture, and the primitive ethnic charm of Umbrian earthenware. Culturally he was brought up on a rather meagre diet of Antonioni and Fellini, and he is probably still quietly in love with Monica Vitti.

Jonathan rationalizes that what he drives is no ordinary means of transport, but a Driver's Car, His macho machine may be falling apart and rusting in peace, but like an Antonioni film, it is high on style, and low on finish; and to him Style is everything. He is one of the few drivers who actually uses his glove-compartment to keep his driving-gloves in; most contain a motley medley of screwed-up parking tickets, half-sucked boiled sweets, an empty nasal-spray, an apple-core and a mysterious bolt that suddenly appeared on the floor-mat, which is never thown away, in case it is vital. In the case of the Lancia, it probably is.

If I kiss you, will you turn into a lay-by?

Young Man's Fancy

DUMPER TRUCK

Mick drives his giant Tonka toy through the traffic in the same way as he elbows his way to the bar on Friday night to order his first of many pints of Guinness. Pedestrians, in the pub and on the streets, have to leap for their lives as he pile-drives through. Traffic islands assume the role of sanctuaries for those lucky and athletic enough to reach them. Mick regards the road as an enormous bowling-alley; he is to the high street what the town-planner is to aesthetics.

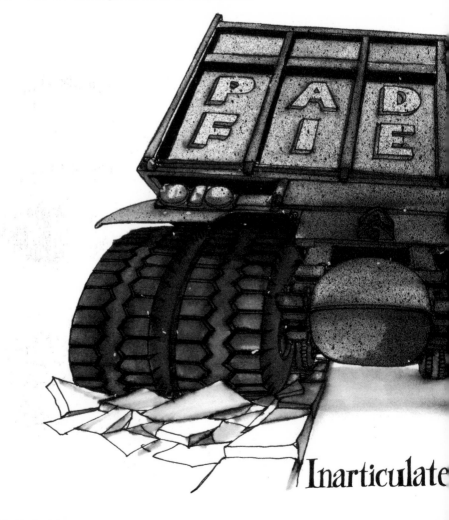

Inarticulate

When not carving up the man-in-the-street, he parks his fully-laden lorry with two wheels on the pavement outside Joe's Greasy Spoon at 8 a.m. Inside Joe's, where cholestoral is measured in hectolitres, Mick is taking on a second load of sausage, egg and chips, with a liberal drenching of brown sauce. After a snout, a perusal of the third and back pages of the Sun, it's back on the road, with a cry of 'Bollards', to terrorize a few more motorists until dinner-time. Dinner usually comprises sausage, egg, chips and beans, and should not be confused with Tea, which is simply sausage, egg and chips.

orry-driver

LONG-DISTANCE LORRY

Although Jack has never eaten a Yorkie Bar or SHED HIS LOAD in the Blackwall Tunnel at seven o'clock on a wet winter's morning, causing misery and mayhem to millions of motorists, he once featured on Capital Radio's Get-u-to-work service; his item was the JACK-KNIFED LORRY at the southern end of the M1/North Circular roundabout (causing misery and mayhem to millions of motorists), and being responsible for a record FOUR-MILE TAILBACK for that stretch of motorway.

Jack can back his 32-ton monster, the size of a large family house, through a gap with a mere six inches to spare each side. He can smoke sixty cigarettes in a day without coughing. Much. He can change a wheel on his own in sub-zero conditions. He can negotiate Customs without speaking one word of Greek, or Serbo Croat. He can't wait to get back to dear old England, where at least they know how to make a decent cup of tea, brew a decent ale ('and none of that fizzy muck they call beer, thank you very much,') and can do a half-decent fry-up. 'There's one thing they're good at, though; they know how to make a decent Chip. Particularly the Belgies. They may not be able to drive, but they certainly can make a good Chip.'

Jack the Knife

TAXI-CAB

Fare-minded

Sid would hardly describe himself as a mastermind; he knows his Knowledge from A to Z, from Abbess Close to Zoffany Street and little else, save who won the 2.15 at Haydock Park. In spite of this, he will readily expound his views on the economic situation, immigration, the Royal Family, and unemployment. He takes great delight in speaking to his fares over one shoulder and through a two-inch gap, so that the poor passenger ends up half-crouching, or sitting on the fold-down seat, to catch the odd word.

'I've had all sorts in the back; film stars, politicians, royalty. I had Cary Grant once. And Tallullah Bankhead. And Bertrand Russell. He was a nice bloke. Couldn't tell me what it was all about, though. I said to him, I said, What's it all about, Bertrand? That stumped him.'

Sid sits hunched over the wheel in his cloth cap and puffy mauve anorak for hours on end, never leaving his cab, waiting for the mythical big-tipping American to hail him outside the Dorchester and ask to be taken to Stratford-upon-Avon. 'Gawd, you see some right Charlies. Look at that wally, doing a U-turn. I ask you. Gerrahtofit, you stupid BERK! Yeah, *and* you, sunshine!'

NEWSPAPER VAN

The chances of *not* being hit by one of these vans are four times more than being struck by lightning. Twice. In the same place. And, as a pedestrian, the chances of being flattened against a wall by a flying bale of Late Editions are no better. Apart from Belgians, embassy Mercedes's, and Cruise missiles, these vans are the vehicles to be avoided the most. In a more enlightened age, they were fitted with black rubber wings, that yielded a little when in contact with metal. Alas for the private motorist, they are now made of the same material as his own beloved car. The newspaper van has only one known enemy – the predatory dumper-truck. This is due entirely to size, and the fact that Mick cares even *less* about damaging his vehicle. However, scraps between these two are rare, as the van is far nippier. They don't call it Fleet street for nothing. So nimble are these lads around town, you could be reading the account of your accident in the Stop Press before the breakdown truck has arrived to tow away the wreckage.

Press on Regardless

CUSTOM CAR

'She's in BEAUTIFUL condition. And cop a gander at those great lines! And just look at that bodywork! Right? And what a GOER! Geddit? She really is a great little performer, know what I mean? Those are her original bumpers, y'know, but I jacked her up myself, if you follow me . . .'

Ford or Saloon

Dave had his friend, Dave the Mill, drop in a 302 Mustang with a Crane Fireball cam, Headman headers, and a Holley 390 four-barrel breathing thru an Offy manifold and exiting out of a pair of Cherry Bombs. Wow. Dave the Spray did the cellulose and metalflake paint-job and Dave the Brush cracked out the pinstriping and graphics. Then all that was needed was a chrome beam axle and four-bar with Pete and Jake micro-flex bushes and the usual Jag rear-end, and 10-inch Rockets to lay a patch at the back. Fun, huh?

Dave has never been the same since Buddy Holly ran out of sky on 3 February 1959 near Mason City, Iowa, and has worn a black shirt ever since. He plays Ritchie Valens and the Big Bopper, too, at full whack through his quad system, and rocks on to Eddy Cochran, Little Richard, Chuck Berry and the BIG DADDY, Elvis. ONE, TWO, THREE FOUR FIVE, ROCK 'N' ROLL IS STILL ALIVE. Dave no longer goes down to Southend, kicking scooters about; instead, he spends his Saturdays cruisin'. Has 'e gorn soft?

UNACCUSTOMED AS I AM...

INDEX